John Lewis
Making Good Trouble

Amanda Jackson Green

Reader Consultants

Dr. Artika R. Tyner
President & CEO Planting People Growing Justice

Cheryl Norman Lane, M.A.Ed.
Classroom Teacher
Chino Valley Unified School District

Jennifer M. Lopez, M.S.Ed., NBCT
Teacher Specialist—History/Social Studies
Norfolk Public Schools

iCivics Consultants

Emma Humphries, Ph.D.
Chief Education Officer

Taylor Davis, M.T.
Director of Curriculum and Content

Natacha Scott, MAT
Director of Educator Engagement

Publishing Credits

Rachelle Cracchiolo, M.S.Ed., *Publisher*
Emily R. Smith, M.A.Ed., *VP of Content Development*
Véronique Bos, *Creative Director*
Dona Herweck Rice, *Senior Content Manager*
Dani Neiley, *Associate Content Specialist*
Fabiola Sepulveda, *Series Designer*

Image Credits: front cover, p.15 bottom Newscom; p.3 LOC (LC-U9- 10380-13); p.4 Getty Images/Steve Schapiro; p.5 US Congress; pp.6–9 Becky Davies; p.10 LOC (LC-USF33-030372-M2); p.11 Getty Images/Bloomberg; p.14 LOC (HABS KY-288); p.15 Getty Images/Smith Collection/Gado; p.16 LOC (LC-DIG-ppmsca-03119); p.17 LOC (LC-USZ62-134434); p.18 Getty Images/Don Cravens; p.19 LOC (LC-USZ62-122988); p.20 LOC (LC-DIG-ppmsc-01270); p.20 bottom, p.21, pp.23–24, p.26 Getty Images/ Bettmann; p.22 Getty Images/Robert W. Kelley; p.25 Everett Collection/Newscom; p.27 Associated Press; p.28 Tami Chappell/REUTERS/Newscom; p.29 The White House; all other images from iStock and/or Shutterstock

Library of Congress Cataloging-in-Publication Data

Names: Green, Amanda Jackson, 1988- author. | iCivics (Organization), consultant.
Title: John Lewis : making good trouble / Amanda Jackson Green.
Description: Huntington Beach, CA : Teacher Created Materials, [2021] |
    "iCivics"--Cover. | Audience: Grades: 2-3 | Summary: "John Lewis had a passion for justice. When he saw wrongdoing, he spoke up. In the face of challenges, he did not back down. His words and courage inspired important change in America"-- Provided by publisher.
Identifiers: LCCN 2021058743 (print) | LCCN 2021058744 (ebook) | ISBN 9781087643014 (paperback) | ISBN 9781087643021 (ebook)
Subjects: LCSH: Lewis, John, 1940-2020--Juvenile literature. | United States. Congress. House--Biography--Juvenile literature. | Legislators--United States--Biography--Juvenile literature. | African American legislators--Biography--Juvenile literature. | Civil rights workers--United States--Biography--Juvenile literature. | Civil rights movements--Southern States--History--20th century--Juvenile literature. |African Americans--Civil rights--Southern States--History--20th century--Juvenile literature.
Classification: LCC E840.8.L43 G74 2021 (print) | LCC E840.8.L43 (ebook) | DDC 328.73/092 [B]--dc23
LC record available at https://lccn.loc.gov/2021058743
LC ebook record available at https://lccn.loc.gov/2021058744

TCM | Teacher Created Materials

5482 Argosy Avenue
Huntington Beach, CA 92649-1039
www.tcmpub.com

ISBN 978-1-0876-4301-4
© 2022 Teacher Created Materials, Inc.

The name "iCivics" and the iCivics logo are registered trademarks of iCivics, Inc.

Table of Contents

Lift Every Voice

From a young age, John Lewis had a strong sense of right and wrong. He believed everyone should be treated with respect. In the presence of injustice, he refused to stay silent. In fact, he felt it was his duty to speak up and get in the way. Lewis often got in trouble for standing up for his values. But he did not back down. He had a vision for a better world. He was set on making it come true.

John Lewis, civil rights activist, age 22

Lewis's passion made him a powerful **civil rights** leader. His tireless quest for **justice** took him to the United States **Congress**. Along the way, he inspired other people to lift their voices too. His memory still inspires.

Representative John Lewis

Jump into Fiction

Good Trouble

It was a crisp September morning in Troy, Alabama. The sun had not yet risen to warm the autumn air as John tiptoed to the chicken coop, schoolbooks clutched in his arms. He knelt to stroke his favorite hen behind the head. "Can you keep a secret, Bitsy? I'm going to school today. Mama and Daddy say they need me to stay and help in the fields. But there is so much I need to learn! I'll be back before you know it."

This is a fictional retelling of a true story from John Lewis's life.

John crept quietly through the darkness toward the farmhouse. There, he plopped down his books and shimmied under the porch. The dust made him sneeze. Tiny pebbles pressed into his hands and knees. He was uncomfortable, but he stayed focused on his goal. His eyes were trained on the dirt road ahead.

It felt like hours passed before the school bus zoomed up the road, kicking up gravel along the way. John shuffled out from his hiding spot and sprinted just in time to catch it.

"Headed to school today?" asked Mr. Jones.

John nodded at the driver and took a seat. Balancing his books on his lap, he brushed the dirt from his knees.

It might be lunchtime before John's parents noticed he was gone. They would be upset. He broke their rules. But the chance to learn was worth the scolding he faced when he got home. "Some trouble is good trouble," John thought as he rested his head against the window for the long journey to the schoolhouse.

Back to Nonfiction

Life on the Farm

John Robert Lewis was born on February 21, 1940, near Troy, Alabama. His parents were Eddie and Willie Mae Lewis. They worked as **sharecroppers**. They did not make much money. But they saved their earnings. Soon, they were able to buy their own farm.

Sharecroppers like Lewis's family work on a farm.

Cotton

In the early 1900s, cotton was the main **export** of the South. The region has a warm climate and rich soil. This makes it an ideal place to grow the crop.

Farming was hard work. Each family member had to do their part. Lewis and his nine siblings had many chores. They fed the animals and cleaned their pens every day. In the spring, they prepared the fields for planting cotton. They harvested the crops in the fall.

Lewis grew up in a home like this one.

Preaching to the Chickens

Lewis was a bright and curious child. At age four, he got a Bible for Christmas. Day and night, he read the book. The stories of brave leaders thrilled Lewis. These heroes spoke up for what was right, even when others disagreed. Some went to jail for their ideas. Still, they were not afraid to challenge harmful rules.

Lewis wanted to be a preacher when he grew up. Dressed in a suit and tie, he often made up speeches and recited them aloud. Someday, he thought, his words and ideas would inspire others too.

Think and Talk

What does "good trouble" mean to you?

Lewis thrived in the classroom. He loved to ask questions and explore new ideas. However, he was not allowed to go to school until he finished his chores. Most days, this meant he did not go at all. But he sometimes broke his parents' rule, sneaking away to learn. He called it "good trouble."

Good Listeners

One of Lewis's main chores was to feed the chickens. He said they made a perfect audience for his speeches. They always listened and never talked back!

Not Equal

One part of school really upset Lewis. Like many towns in the South, Troy was **segregated**. Black children and white children went to separate schools. White students got new books each year. They had a beautiful playground and plenty of space to run at recess. Lewis and his Black classmates got old, tattered books. They had a cramped schoolhouse with dirt floors. The students were treated differently because of their skin color. Lewis knew this was unfair.

Lewis attended a segregated school like this one.

At home, Lewis shared his concerns with his parents. They said that was just the way things were. They told him to keep quiet and stay out of trouble. Lewis thought there must be a better way. Again, he imagined the heroes from his Bible and the "good trouble" they got into.

A boy uses a segregated water fountain.

Read, My Child

Lewis loved books. His teacher encouraged him to read as often as he could. As an adult, he wrote three graphic novels about his life. He hoped his story would inspire children to use their voices for good.

A Different Way

When Lewis was 11, he took a trip with his uncle to visit relatives in Buffalo, New York. Buffalo was very different from Troy. Black people and white people lived in the same areas. They went to the same stores and diners. Many children attended **integrated** schools. Lewis was amazed! He had never seen anything like this before.

These children attend an integrated school.

Brave children are jeered as they line up to enter their integrated school.

He went back home a few weeks later. Troy was still the same as Lewis had left it. But he began to see it with new eyes. He knew what was possible. African Americans could have the same rights as white people. Lewis wanted to help make that change. But he was not sure how.

The Great Migration

Starting in the early 1900s, millions of Black people left the South. They wanted to get away from **Jim Crow laws**. In the North, they also found better jobs and homes. This movement was known as the Great Migration.

Dr. King's Path

In 1954, Lewis started high school. That year, the **U.S. Supreme Court** made a big decision. The judges said it was not fair to separate schools by race. States must end school segregation. This news thrilled Lewis. Finally, all children in Troy would enjoy the same schools! But the change was slow to come. Some leaders in the South ignored the court's ruling. They thought Black people should not be equal to white people. Lewis felt helpless.

One day, Lewis heard a preacher on the radio. His name was Dr. Martin Luther King Jr. He said everyone should speak up when they see others being mistreated. King felt it was a **civic duty**. This idea excited Lewis. After all, he had a voice, and he knew how to use it.

Pulpits to Picket Lines

In the South, churches were the center of Black social life. Civil rights leaders used churches too. They often met in churches to share their problems and ideas for change.

Dr. King speaks to news reporters.

Think and Talk

Why is Dr. King included in a book about John Lewis?

A Rising Leader

At the age of 17, Lewis went to college in Nashville, Tennessee. There he met a preacher named Jim Lawson. Lawson held meetings at a local church. He called for **nonviolent protest**.

John Lewis

Lewis was inspired. He planned **sit-ins**. He and other students sat at the whites-only counters of diners. Waiters would not serve them. White people hit them and spit in their faces. Police took the Black students to jail. The students stayed calm. After months, their protests worked. Nashville lawmakers ended segregation.

Protesters peacefully gather at a lunch counter.

Lewis now knew the power of protest. He joined a group called the Freedom Riders. They rode buses through the South. They wanted to end segregation on buses. People beat them. Police arrested them. Lewis and the others kept going.

Lewis is arrested for his work with the Freedom Riders.

First Amendment

The First Amendment covers a few legal rights. It gives people freedom of speech and more. People cannot be jailed for sharing their opinions. Americans can use free speech to make changes. Peaceful protest is one way.

Leading for Change

His work in Nashville earned Lewis fame. People asked him to help create more change. Lewis helped plan a huge march in 1963. Around 250,000 people traveled to Washington, DC. They came from all over the country. Leaders such as Dr. King spoke to the crowd. They called for equal access to jobs. They spoke against unfair voting laws. They asked for an end to Jim Crow laws. It was here that Dr. King gave his famous "I Have a Dream" speech.

Lewis (front left) marches with King and others for civil rights.

Lewis speaks at the March on Washington.

Lewis was the youngest speaker there. He was 23 years old. Lewis talked about the times he was jailed. He said it was a small price to pay for justice. The March on Washington inspired lawmakers to act. They soon passed the Civil Rights Act. The law promised equal voting rights for everyone. It ended legal segregation. Lewis again saw the power of his voice.

Planes, Trains, and...Roller Skates?

People came from all around to the March on Washington. Ledger Smith took a unique path. He traveled on roller skates! His trip was about 685 miles (1,102 kilometers) long and took 10 days.

More Good Trouble

Lewis become a well-known leader. He traveled from city to city to give speeches. He spoke about civil rights. In 1965, Lewis led a march to protest unfair voting laws. These laws blocked Black people from voting.

Marchers and state troopers at the Edmund Pettus Bridge in March 1965.

Cast Your Ballot

The United States is a **democracy**. People choose their leaders. They make this choice by voting. Citizens in some states also vote on certain laws. Voting is a way to make your voice heard.

Officers beat Lewis on "Bloody Sunday" at the planned march from Selma to Montgomery.

The marchers set out from a church in Selma, Alabama. Soon, they reached a bridge. A group of state troopers blocked the bridge. They refused to let the marchers pass. The troopers attacked the protestors with clubs and whips. Fifty-eight people were sent to the hospital. Lewis was one of them. A trooper had hit him on the head with a club. The force cracked Lewis's skull.

News channels shared videos of the attack. Americans were angry. They demanded justice. President Lyndon Johnson answered their call. He signed the Voting Rights Act. The law banned **literacy tests** that were designed to keep Black people from voting. It made other important changes too. Lewis was hopeful. His trouble had been worthwhile.

Serving in Congress

Over the next two decades, Lewis continued to speak about voting. He said it was the best tool for change. He asked everyone to vote. In 1986, he ran for Congress as a representative from Georgia. This time, he asked others to vote for him. They did. He won the election. Then, he won 16 more times!

For 32 years, Lewis worked in Congress. He helped write hundreds of new laws. He fought to protect citizens' freedoms and to help those who did not have a lot. And he spoke up when he felt the actions of other leaders were wrong.

John Lewis is elected to Congress.

U.S. Congress

The United States Congress is made up of two chambers. They are called the Senate and the House of Representatives. Each state elects two senators. The House has 435 members. States with more people get more House seats.

In 2009, Barack Obama became president of the United States. He was the first Black person in the role. Lewis was thrilled. As a child, he dreamed of a better life for Black people. Obama said Lewis made it possible. He thanked Lewis for standing up for fairness.

Lewis and his wife Lillian celebrate his success.

A Legacy of Peace

Lewis did not become a preacher like he dreamed as a boy. But he found another way to use his voice to change the world. He inspired others with his words. He faced struggles and danger with courage. And he did it all with peace and kindness.

Lewis died on July 17, 2020. He was 80 years old. In his final days, he wrote a letter to all Americans. The letter was published in a newspaper so everyone could read it. In it, Lewis encouraged people to speak up for their beliefs. He urged them to follow the way of peace. And he told them not to be afraid to get into good trouble.

Lewis with leaders from "both sides of the aisle"

A High Honor

President Obama gave Lewis the **Presidential Medal of Freedom**. He praised Lewis for using his voice. Lewis paved the way for others, Obama said. Obama hoped more people would speak up for change too.

Glossary

civic duty—a duty people have to serve society

civil rights—the rights that all people should have regardless of things such as religion, race, or gender

Congress—the U.S. Senate and the House of Representatives

democracy—a form of government in which people vote for their leaders

export—an item that is sold to other regions or countries

integrated—open or available to all races

Jim Crow laws—U.S. laws that allowed or required segregation between races and discrimination against Black citizens

justice—fair and equal treatment under the law

literacy tests—tests of reading skills that were often made to oppress Black people

nonviolent protest—to peacefully state disagreement with a law or policy, usually in large and organized groups of people

Presidential Medal of Freedom—an award given by the U.S. president to those who made significant contributions to the country

segregated—separated into groups according to race, as a matter of practice or official policy

sharecroppers—farmers who raise crops for landowners and are paid part of the sales

sit-ins—protests that involve peacefully sitting in a place

U.S. Supreme Court—the highest court in the nation

Index

Civics in Action

When people want to cause changes, they use their rights to take action. They may even make "good trouble." They may write letters or make posters. They may make speeches like John Lewis did. Always, their actions show what is important to them. They want things to be fair for everyone.

1. Think about an issue taking place today.

2. Think about why this issue is important to you.

3. Write a speech or make a poster to share your thoughts about this issue.

4. Give your speech or share the poster you made.

5. What change do you hope will happen?